UP IN THE AIR

Written by **Zoë Armstrong**

Illustrated by **Sara ugolotti**

Written by Zoë Armstrong
Illustrated by Sara Ugolotti
Editor Kat Teece
Designer Sonny Flynn
Jacket Designer Elle Ward
US Editor Jane Perlmutter
US Senior Editor Shannon Beatty
Managing Editor Jonathan Melmoth
Managing Art Editor Diane Peyton Jones
Picture Researcher Sakshi Saluja
Production Controller Barbara Ossowska
Production Editor Abi Maxwell
Senior DTP Designer Jagtar Singh
Creative Director Helen Senior
Publishing Director Sarah Larter

Consultants Dr. Ryan Neely III and Steve Setford

First American Edition, 2021
Published in the United States by DK Publishing
1450 Broadway, Suite 801, New York, NY 10018

CONTENTS

21 22 23 24 25 10 9 8 7 6 5 4 3 2 1
001–321270–Jun/2021

Published in Great Britain by Dorling Kindersley Limited

A catalog record for this book
is available from the Library of Congress.
ISBN 978-0-7440-3324-3

DK books are available at special discounts when purchased in
bulk for sales promotions, premiums, fund-raising,
or educational use. For details, contact: DK Publishing
Special Markets, 1450 Broadway, Suite 801,
New York, NY 10018 SpecialSales@dk.com

Printed and bound in China

For the curious
www.dk.com

Flitting across the sky

With a flash of blue feathers, a jay flits between the trees. Jays can mimic the sounds of other animals – even humans! Discover more brilliant birds on pages 20–27.

Bird calls fill the air.

WHAT CAN YOU SEE?

Up in the air, nature floats and flutters and drifts and dazzles. There are sounds and colors and all kinds of creatures. What do you see up there?

Fluttering past

A comma butterfly searches for stinging nettles on which to lay her eggs. Turn to pages 16–19 for more butterflies.

Honeysuckle

Flowers release perfume into the breeze.

Nesting in trees

This cup-shaped nest belongs to a song thrush. Look at nests big, small, and strangely shaped on pages 26–27.

Starlings

Clouds and birds make shapes in the sky.

Changing colors

The sky changes color as light is filtered through Earth's atmosphere. Learn more about the shades of the sky on pages 6–7.

Catching prey

Static electricity makes this spider's web spring toward passing prey, like hair sticking to a rubbed balloon. Find the orb-weaver spider on page 53.

Fox

THROUGH THE DAY

The sun rises over the horizon. It brings light and warmth, and gives energy to plants so they can make their food. A new day has begun.

Animals that are active during the day but rest at night are called diurnal. Most birds are diurnal.

The horizon is the point at which the land or sea appears to meet the sky.

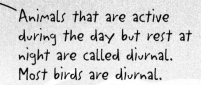

Sunrise

Sunlight is made of many colors. The sky can look yellow or pink at sunrise and sunset because some colors of light are scattered by the air and other floating particles before they reach your eye.

Sun path

As the Earth rotates each day, the sun seems to follow an arc-shaped path across the sky. The path changes through the year, as the Earth orbits (moves around) the sun.

Poppies

Poppies open their petals with the morning light. Poppies are heliotropic—they track the path of the sun from east to west.

Sun compass

Many animals use the sun like a compass to find their way. Birds, butterflies, bees, reptiles, and ants use the sun's position in the sky as part of their navigation systems.

Summer
Spring or fall
Winter

Animals that are active at dawn and dusk are called crepuscular.

Sunflowers

Young sunflowers are heliotropic, like poppies. But the mature flowers point east throughout the day.

Evening flowers

As the sun sets, jasmine flowers release a sweet smell. Some flowers are more fragrant at night to lure nocturnal insects. The insects spread pollen, which allows the plants to make seeds.

WHAT IS AIR?

Air is all around us, but we don't see it. It fills our lungs, though we don't always feel it. Air supports life in plants and animals. But what exactly is it?

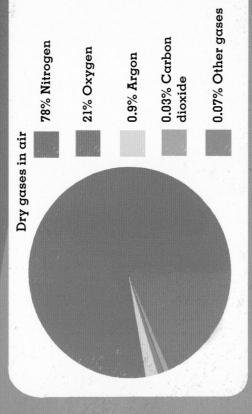

Dry gases in air

- 78% Nitrogen
- 21% Oxygen
- 0.9% Argon
- 0.03% Carbon dioxide
- 0.07% Other gases

Stratosphere

The atmosphere

We often use the word "air" to talk about Earth's atmosphere. This is a protective layer of gases. It holds onto heat, so we don't get too cold.

Dry and wet

Air is mostly a mixture of gases. Nitrogen and oxygen make up 99 percent of the dry gases in the atmosphere. Air also contains up to 5 percent water vapor, which is water in the form of a wet gas.

A layer of ozone gas protects us from the sun's harmful rays.

Troposphere

Earth's atmosphere has five different layers rising up into outer space. The layer we live in is called the troposphere—this is where most of the air is!

Air contains tiny particles, such as pollen and sea salt, called aerosols. Some aerosols can harm our health.

Pollution

Many power stations and vehicles are powered by burning fossil fuels. This releases extra carbon dioxide and other gases into the air, which are types of pollution that cause the Earth to heat up.

Breathing in

You breathe in air because your body needs oxygen to keep working. You breathe out to get rid of carbon dioxide. Plants do this too, but they also use carbon dioxide to make food.

When plants make their food, they take in carbon dioxide from the air and release oxygen.

How air moves

Warm air rises and colder air sinks. When a pocket of warm air rises, it leaves behind an area of low pressure. This is like a space that colder air rushes into, as wind.

UP, UP, AND AWAY

The air is a thriving ecosystem, teeming with life. In addition to birds and bats, there are millions of tiny insects and organisms swirling high above our heads.

Microbes

Bacteria, viruses, and fungal spores can be carried thousands of feet up into Earth's atmosphere. Some even float across continents.

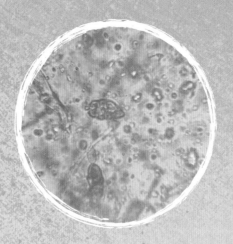

Damselflies

Some species of damselfly fly high into the air to be swept away by strong winds. Rambur's forktail damselflies have been found on oil rigs miles out at sea in the Gulf of Mexico.

Thermals

The sun doesn't heat the Earth evenly— sunny places get hotter than shady areas. This creates columns of rising warm air, called thermals, that whisk tiny life-forms up into the atmosphere.

Aeroplankton

Aeroplankton are tiny life forms that float through the air, drifting and swirling with the breeze. They are the air's equivalent of the plankton that float through the oceans.

Aphids

Aphids often migrate hundreds of miles on the breeze. Young winged aphids can fly around 2,000 ft (600 m) into the air to be whisked away by the wind.

Ballooning

Many spiders float over long distances. The spider points its abdomen up, then casts out long strands of silk, which catch the breeze and carry the spider away.

In addition to riding the wind, the ballooning spiders are carried by Earth's electric field.

Bumblebees

These have been found more than 18,000 ft (5,500 m) above sea level—on the slopes of the world's tallest mountain, Mount Everest.

13

Flies

Most flying insects have two pairs of wings. But, instead of back wings, flies have tiny, club-shaped balancing organs, for super-aerobatic flight!

The eyes of a dragonfly wrap around its head. They can spot prey from nearly every angle.

Flies are an important part of the food chain, providing nourishment for many animals, such as birds.

Dragonflies

Shimmering dragonflies dart over lakes and rivers. The largest living dragonfly has a wingspan of up to 6.7 in (17 cm), but prehistoric dragonflies had wingspans just over four times this size!

One of the biggest flying insects is the Hercules beetle, which can grow to around 6.7 in (17 cm) long.

Beetles

The wings of a beetle are folded up beneath shiny, protective wing cases, called elytra. Some male beetles have body parts that look like pincers or horns, which they use for fighting.

FLYING INSECTS

Winged insects may buzz, swarm, or hover in the air. They eat pests, pollinate plants, and provide food for birds and other creatures.

Locusts

These grasshoppers sometimes form swarms as wide as a city. Swarms can fly for hundreds of miles, wreaking havoc as the locusts eat their way through food crops.

Mosquitoes

Mosquitoes feed on nectar, but females of some types of mosquito also need animal blood to make their eggs. These mosquitoes can spread diseases when they bite.

Colorful wing cases warn predators that ladybugs taste very bitter.

Ladybugs flap their wings about 85 times every second.

BEES

The sound of buzzing coming from a tree might suggest a beehive! There are about 20,000 known species of bees in the world, but only a few species make honey.

This reserve of honey will nourish the colony over the winter.

Honeybees transport pellets of pollen on their back legs, like saddlebags. They carry nectar inside their bodies.

Gathering food

Bees fly from flower to flower, sucking up a sweet juice called nectar and gathering pollen to eat. Many plants rely on bees to spread their pollen in order to reproduce.

Making honey

Back at the hive, honeybees mix the nectar with a chemical called an enzyme, which is made inside their bodies. The bees pass the mixture from mouth to mouth and slowly it turns to honey.

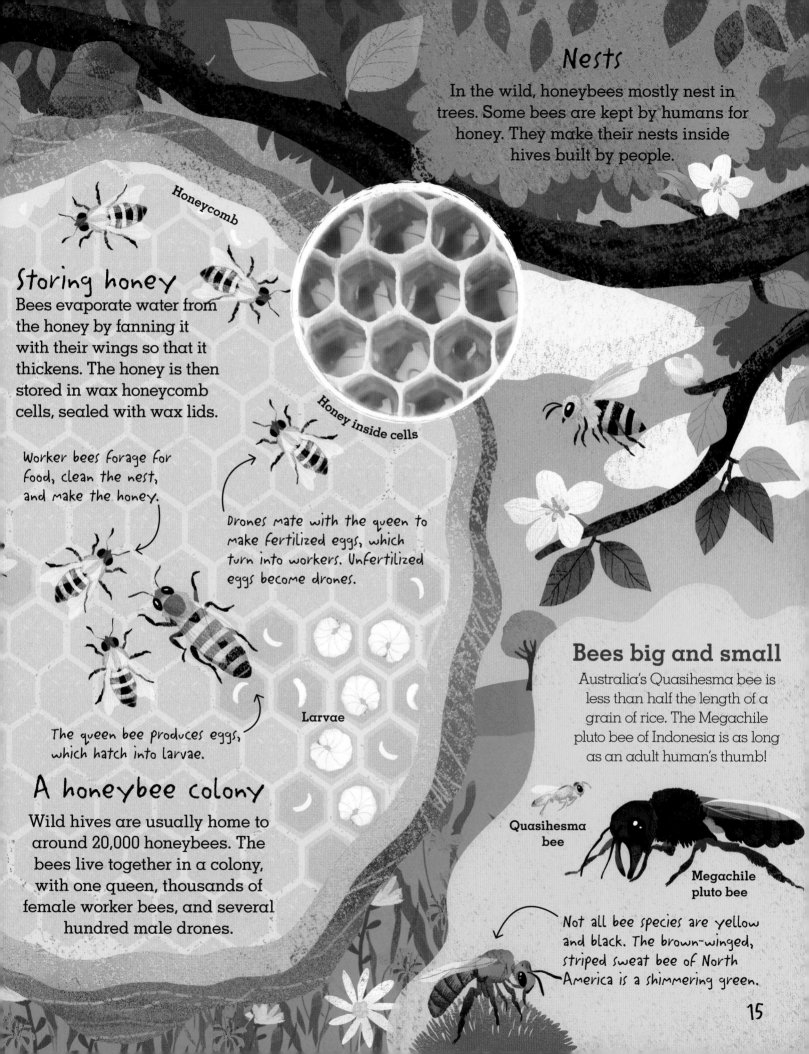

Nests

In the wild, honeybees mostly nest in trees. Some bees are kept by humans for honey. They make their nests inside hives built by people.

Honeycomb

Honey inside cells

Storing honey

Bees evaporate water from the honey by fanning it with their wings so that it thickens. The honey is then stored in wax honeycomb cells, sealed with wax lids.

Worker bees forage for food, clean the nest, and make the honey.

Drones mate with the queen to make fertilized eggs, which turn into workers. Unfertilized eggs become drones.

The queen bee produces eggs, which hatch into larvae.

Larvae

A honeybee colony

Wild hives are usually home to around 20,000 honeybees. The bees live together in a colony, with one queen, thousands of female worker bees, and several hundred male drones.

Bees big and small

Australia's Quasihesma bee is less than half the length of a grain of rice. The Megachile pluto bee of Indonesia is as long as an adult human's thumb!

Quasihesma bee

Megachile pluto bee

Not all bee species are yellow and black. The brown-winged, striped sweat bee of North America is a shimmering green.

15

CHANGING SHAPE

A caterpillar transforms into a winged butterfly or moth, in a process called metamorphosis. Crawling, hanging, or fluttering—look out for every stage...

Caterpillar

A tiny caterpillar hatches. It eats its eggshell, then it begins to eat the leaves. As it grows, it sheds its skin up to five times—this is called molting.

Monarch butterfly

Each year, millions of monarch butterflies make amazing migrations in the fall. They fly thousands of miles south, from Canada and northern US, to Mexico.

Monarch butterflies only feed on the milkweed plant.

Some species lay eggs singly, while others lay many at a time.

Egg

A female butterfly or moth lays an egg on a leaf. She chooses a plant her caterpillar will like to eat.

Pupa

At the final molt, a hard casing
forms around its body, and the caterpillar
becomes a pupa. A butterfly's casing is
called a chrysalis. A moth caterpillar spins
a cocoon of silk around itself, instead.

Inside, the
pupa is forming
wings, legs,
and antennae.

Adult

After a while, the chrysalis or cocoon
breaks open and a butterfly or moth
emerges. At first its wings are wet and
crinkled, but soon the new insect
is ready to fly.

Butterflies fly during the
day. Moths normally (but
not always) fly at night.

Butterflies and
moths are important
pollinators.

17

Chalkhill blue butterfly

This butterfly flits over chalky grasslands in Europe. The caterpillars make a sugary substance that ants like to eat. In return, the ants protect the caterpillars and chrysalises.

Peacock butterfly

The peacock butterfly of Europe and Asia has eyelike markings. The false eyes trick predators into thinking they are facing a much larger animal.

Madagascan sunset moth

This moth is unusual because it flies during the day. It is often mistaken for a butterfly because of its beautiful colors, which warn predators that it is toxic (poisonous) to eat.

Black-and-white coloring says to predators "Stay away, I'm not good to eat."

The pattern is often slightly different on each wing.

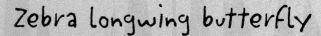

Zebra longwing butterfly

In South and Central America, the caterpillars of this butterfly feast on passion-flower leaves, which are toxic to other animals. The leaves make the caterpillars and butterflies poisonous to predators!

Elephant hawk-moth

Pink and olive-gold elephant hawk-moths are common in Europe. They sip nectar from honeysuckle and other sweet-smelling flowers at night.

Lunar moth

The "tails" of a lunar moth's wings twirl as it flies. This confuses hunting bats, which often strike at the tails instead of the body, and the moth can escape with its life!

The markings at the wing tips look like snake heads, which may confuse or scare off predators.

Atlas moth

With a wingspan of up to 10.6 in (27 cm), the Asian atlas moth is one of the largest insects on Earth. It does all its eating as a caterpillar, because the adult moth has no mouthparts!

Silk moth

The caterpillars of the silk moth are known as silkworms. To make cocoons, they spin thread called silk. Humans collect the thread and weave it into smooth silk fabric.

BUTTERFLIES AND MOTHS

Some butterflies and moths are dully colored and small to hide from sight. But others have bright colors and patterns to attract mates, fool predators, or to tell other animals that they are poisonous.

Forces of flight

A force is a push or a pull on an object. There are four forces that act on a bird when it flies...

TAKING FLIGHT

Birds fly to find food and places to raise their young. They can escape predators as they flap and glide and soar across the sky. There are many ways to fly...

Weight, as the force of gravity pulls the bird downward.

Thrust, as the bird is pushed forward by flapping its wings.

Drag, as the bird is held back by resistance from the air.

Lift, as the difference in air pressure above and below the flapping wings pulls the bird upward.

Adapted for flight

Birds have special features to help them overcome gravity and move through the air. These include smooth, lightweight feathers, powerful wings, and hollow bones.

A bird has a curved, streamlined shape. This reduces drag, as the air slips past.

Getting airborne

Many birds launch themselves into the air by leaping from the ground or off a high perch. Some large birds, such as flamingos, need a takeoff run to get into the sky.

There's safety in numbers. Flying as a flock helps guard against predators—with more eyes to look out for danger.

Bounding

After short bursts of flapping, many small birds fold away their wings, and sail through the air. As they start to descend, they put on another burst of flapping. This "bounding" flight saves energy and reduces drag.

Murmurations

Great swirling, swooping, shifting shapes are formed in the sky when thousands of starlings fly together in a murmuration. These aerial displays happen at sunset in winter.

Hovering

Some birds hover in a single spot by beating their wings very fast. Hummingbirds are the fastest flappers—ninety times a second is not unusual!

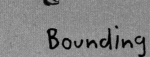

The hummingbird gets its name from the sound made by its wings.

Gliding and soaring

Birds can save energy by stretching their wings out and gliding through the air without flapping. Gliding on a rising current of air is known as soaring.

21

Navigation

Birds find their way using the position of the sun and the stars, the Earth's magnetic field, and landmarks, such as mountains. Smells offer clues too!

Swallows that breed in Britain during the summer fly to southern Africa for the winter.

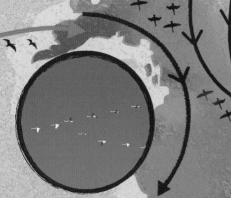

Tundra swans

Pelicans, geese, and tundra swans migrate in a V shape. This helps them move through the air more easily. Tundra swans fly between the Arctic and the US's East and West coasts.

Why migrate?

Migration is all about survival. Birds make these treacherous voyages so that they have food and warmth during the winter, and suitable nesting spots in the summer.

TRAVELING BIRDS

Each year, many birds make epic journeys through the sky. They fly across continents and back again with the changing seasons. This is called migration.

Alpine swifts

Alpine swifts can spend six months in the air without landing. They drink raindrops, eat flying insects, and sleep while airborne as they soar between Europe and Africa.

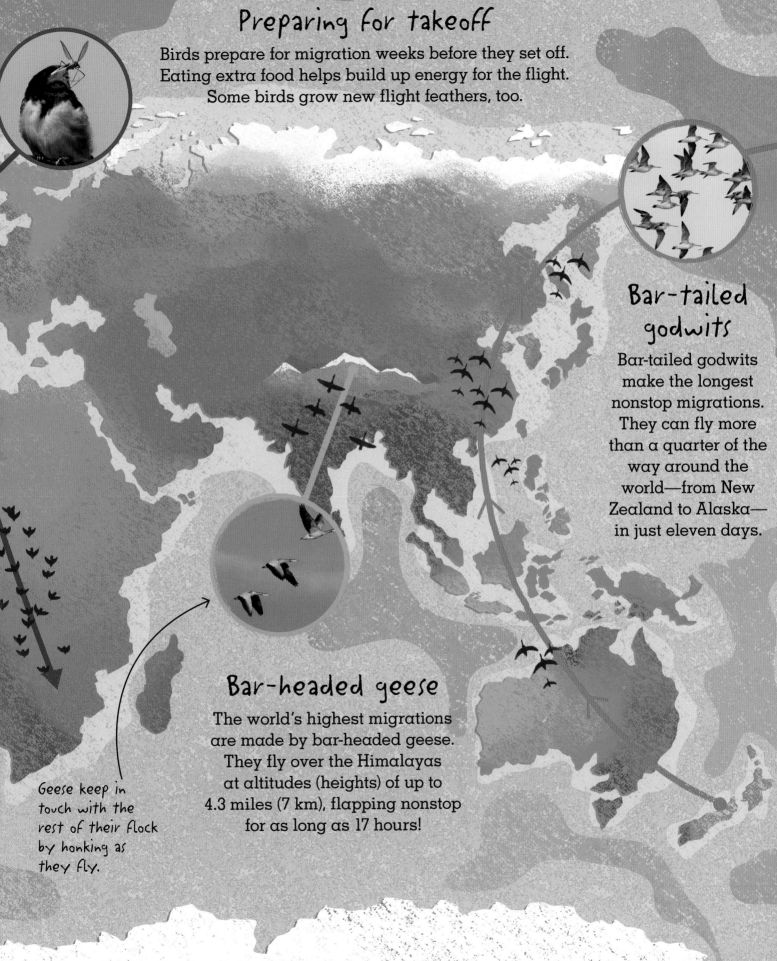

Preparing for takeoff

Birds prepare for migration weeks before they set off.
Eating extra food helps build up energy for the flight.
Some birds grow new flight feathers, too.

Bar-tailed godwits

Bar-tailed godwits make the longest nonstop migrations. They can fly more than a quarter of the way around the world—from New Zealand to Alaska— in just eleven days.

Bar-headed geese

The world's highest migrations are made by bar-headed geese. They fly over the Himalayas at altitudes (heights) of up to 4.3 miles (7 km), flapping nonstop for as long as 17 hours!

Geese keep in touch with the rest of their flock by honking as they fly.

BIRDSONG

Songbirds fill the air with music. They sing to attract a mate and defend their territories. Their complex voice boxes allow them to make extraordinary sounds...

Veer veer veer

Veery

This shy little songbird sings its heart out in the woods and forests of North and South America. It has a spiraling, flutelike song.

Whistle whistler

American robin

The cheerful song of the American robin bounces merrily along. These are often the first songbirds to be heard at dawn.

Warble warble

Nightingale

The nightingale has a powerful voice. Its song whistles, warbles, and bubbles at night, and also during the day.

Whistle whistle

Blackbird

Blackbirds sing a sweet melody late into the evening. These are among the most common songbirds in the UK.

More than half of the world's bird species are songbirds.

The dawn chorus

This good-morning group song begins with the first glimmer of sunlight. It grows from a few calls to a cacophony of singing and squawking.

A bird singing at dawn

Wood lark

Wood larks sing their lilting, sorrowful song as they make circles in the sky across Europe, western Asia, and North Africa.

Lu-lu-lu

Chinese thrush

The Chinese thrush sings its lovely repeating melody, loud and clear, around forests in China and north Vietnam.

Whistle whistle whistle

House sparrow

The simple, chirping song of the noisy little house sparrow can be heard all year round in many parts of the world.

Chirrup chirrup

Pallas's leaf warbler

Pallas's leaf warblers sing powerful medleys of whistles and warbles from the tops of tall trees in China, eastern Siberia, and Mongolia.

Tirrit-tirrt

25

Ruby-throated hummingbird

Female ruby-throated hummingbirds build cup-shaped nests with spider silk, thistledown, and dandelion fluff. They disguise the nest with lichen and moss.

These little nests are found in eastern North America.

HOMES UP HIGH

Nestling between branches or dangling in the air, a treetop nest is a safe shelter away from predators. Many birds build intricate homes, where they take care of their eggs and chicks.

The nests can be more than 20 ft (6 m) wide!

Sociable weaver

In southern Africa, sociable weavers build huge nests, where up to a hundred families live. They use grass, twigs, plant fluff, and fur.

Building a nest

Many birds build their nests over several days, to prepare for laying eggs. They use their beaks to transport material and form the structure.

1. Materials are gathered. Dry grass, twigs, and leaves are used by many birds to weave basket-shaped nests.

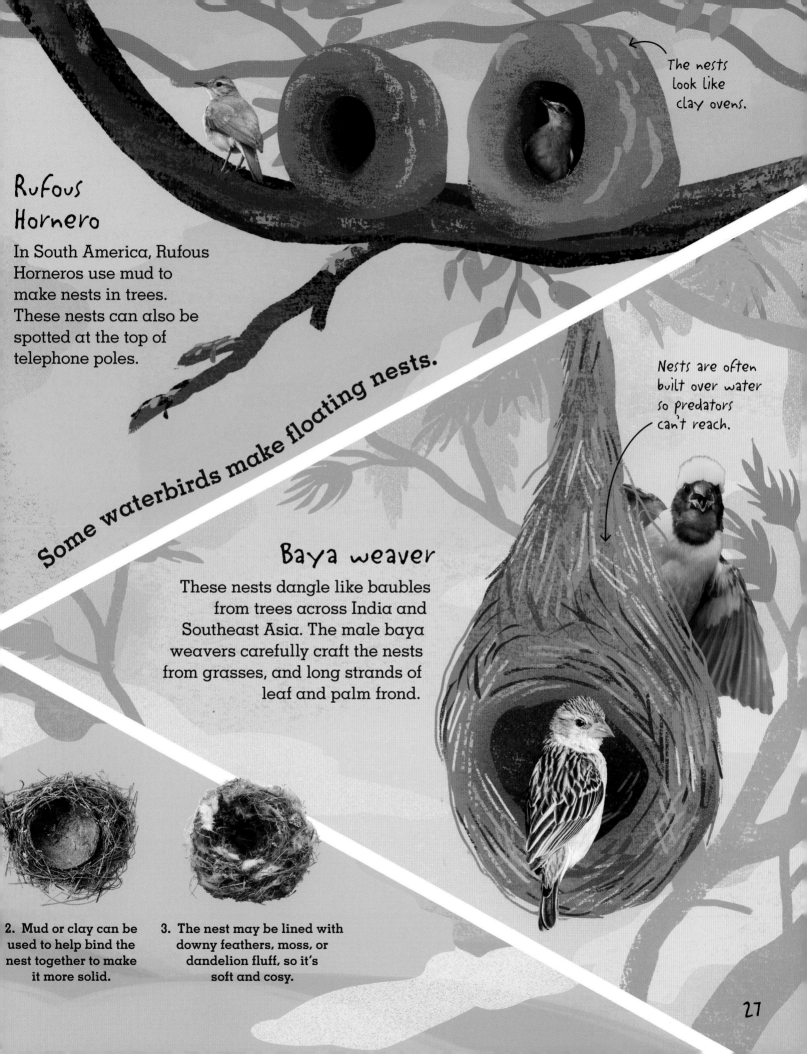

The nests look like clay ovens.

Rufous Hornero

In South America, Rufous Horneros use mud to make nests in trees. These nests can also be spotted at the top of telephone poles.

Some waterbirds make floating nests.

Nests are often built over water so predators can't reach.

Baya weaver

These nests dangle like baubles from trees across India and Southeast Asia. The male baya weavers carefully craft the nests from grasses, and long strands of leaf and palm frond.

2. Mud or clay can be used to help bind the nest together to make it more solid.

3. The nest may be lined with downy feathers, moss, or dandelion fluff, so it's soft and cosy.

TALL TREE TRUNK

A trunk is the stem of a tree. It reaches up into the air, growing wider and stronger as the tree gets taller. Its nooks and crannies are full of life.

Home in a hole

This deer mouse has made a nest in a tree hollow. Deer mice happily scramble up trees to reach food, such as insects and fungi.

Some birds use pieces of lichen as part of their nests.

Different trees have different textures and colors of bark.

Silver birch

The tree's skin

Bark is like a skin. It stops the tree from drying out. It also protects the trunk from extreme temperatures, animals, and diseases.

Growing lichen

Silvers and yellows, oranges and greens, lichens grow in patterns on the bark. They are formed of fungi and algae, working as a team.

Tree rings

If it has to be cut down, a tree's age can be discovered by counting the rings of growth inside its trunk. There is one ring for each year of its life.

Woolly aphid

Seeping sap

Sap is a sugary fluid that carries nourishment around the tree. If a tree is damaged, sap can bleed out until the wound has healed.

Branches can break in strong winds or under heavy snow, or from growing too heavy.

Strange fungus

Jelly-ear fungus grows on dying branches of trees. It is rubbery, gelatinous (jellylike), and shaped like human ears!

Ants and aphids

Wood ants eat honeydew—a sweet liquid made by aphids. The ants protect the small insects in return for honeydew.

29

TREETOP ANIMALS

Rustling through leaves, tapping on bark, or taking a treetop nap, some animals spend most of their lives up in the branches. We call creatures that live in trees "arboreal."

Great spotted woodpecker

This shy bird hammers its beak on hollow branches to mark its territory—about 20 times a second! The drumming sound echoes around forests in Europe, Asia, and North Africa.

The great spotted woodpecker nests in a hole that it carves out of the tree with its strong beak.

Koala

The koala lives a solitary life, mostly munching leaves in Australia's eucalyptus forests. Koalas are marsupials—their babies are carried in a snug pouch for the first six months of their life.

It takes a lot of energy to digest eucalyptus, so a koala spends about 20 hours a day sleeping in its tree.

The woodpecker picks insects off bark, and drills into the wood to pull out grubs with its sticky tongue.

Young pine martens start to explore outside their den at about six-weeks old.

European pine marten

These mammals make dens in natural tree nooks, or holes made by other creatures. Sometimes they take over the nests of squirrels or birds. They leap between branches, chasing their prey.

Claws help the pine marten grip the bark as it climbs. Its claws are tucked away for running on the ground.

Pine martens are hunters. They eat birds, insects, and small mammals, such as voles and squirrels.

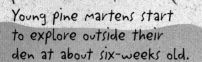

Bank vole

To scamper down a trunk headfirst, a squirrel can rotate its ankles so its paws are pointing backward, to grip the bark better.

Squirrels

Squirrel species are found leaping through trees on every continent, apart from Australia and Antarctica. A squirrel's nest is called a drey. It is made from twigs, leaves, bark, and grass.

Squirrels eat berries, nuts, fungi, seeds, and even birds' eggs.

THE SEASONS

A deciduous tree transforms with the seasons. Colors change and leaves are blown from branches, then new buds sprout and grow. A lot can happen in a year in the life of a tree.

Spring

Branches are dotted with buds, ready to unfurl new leaves. Blossoms attract insects to help with pollination, so the trees can make their seeds.

Bees and other insects buzz from bloom to bloom, carrying pollen as they go.

A wood pigeon tucks into young leaves.

Most growth stops during winter, to save energy.

Bare branches help the tree conserve water, which would otherwise escape as water vapor from leaves.

Winter

The tree has entered a dormant phase, which is a bit like sleeping. Its leaves have fallen and sugar has moved down to be stored in its roots until spring.

Chaffinches come from colder Nordic countries to spend winter in the UK, doubling the usual population.

Summer

The tree is now covered in leaves and teeming with life. It has fruit swelling and ripening on its branches.

Photosynthesis

Leaves use water drawn up through the roots, carbon dioxide from the air, and sunlight to make sugar to feed the tree. Oxygen is also made in this process.

Trees grow quickly in both spring and summer.

Leaves are packed with green chlorophyll, a substance that absorbs energy from the sun.

With less sunlight, leaves stop making food and change color as chlorophyll disappears.

Gusts of wind leave branches nearly bare as the tree sheds its leaves.

Squirrels store nuts and fungi to eat during the colder months, when food is harder to find.

Fall

Leaves turn brilliant shades of red and gold. Fruit falls and seeds begin to scatter, caught by the wind or carried off by birds and other animals.

33

TRAVELING SEEDS

Floating, gliding, and spinning through the air, seeds scattered by breezes find new places to grow. With luck they will land on fertile ground.

Helicopter seeds

Sycamore seeds have delicate wings attached. These allow them to spin away from their parent tree, like tiny helicopters twirling in the breeze.

Dispersal

For survival, seeds must spread out, away from their parent plant, so they don't have to compete for space, water, and light. This is called dispersal.

Some seeds are carried by streams or rivers to new growing spots.

Light and fluffy

Cottonwood trees produce masses of seeds with fluffy, cottonlike coverings that catch the breeze. They can drift and float for miles.

Exploding seedpods

Some seeds are sent whizzing off by the force of an exploding seedpod. Gorse pods go POP as they open after drying out, flinging seeds to better growing spots.

The male catkins release yellow pollen between winter and spring.

Wind pollination

Pollen—which many plants produce in order to make seeds—drifts through the air, too. Hazelnut trees release pollen from male catkins, to be carried by the wind to the smaller female flowers.

Many seeds are light, and shaped to catch the breeze.

Javan cucumber

The seeds of the Javan cucumber vine move through the air like butterflies. Their huge, winged casings are wider than your hand, and shaped to help the seeds swirl over tropical forests.

Animals and seeds

Birds, bats, and other creatures swallow seeds as they munch on fruit. The seeds are carried off inside the animal's stomach, and dropped to the ground when it poops.

When a seed begins to sprout and grow, we say it has germinated.

Tiny parachutes

Dandelion seeds are suspended below tiny, fluffy parachutes, which catch the air to help them float. A puff of breath or a gust of wind carries the seeds away.

Dandelion

35

Olives

Olives are the fruit of olive trees that grow around the Mediterranean. They start out green, and darken to black or brown.

FRUIT

Fruit is the part of a flowering plant that contains the seeds. It protects the seeds until they are ready to be spread, by animals eating the fruit.

Olive

Wild cherry

Lemon

Banana

36 Fig

Pomegranate

NUTS

True nuts are a type of hard fruit. But many of the things we think of as nuts are actually dried seeds that are good to eat, called culinary nuts.

Chestnuts

Chestnuts are true nuts. They are the fruit of the European chestnut tree, wrapped in a prickly casing.

Walnut
(culinary nut)

Chestnut

Pistachio
(culinary nut)

Cashew
(culinary nut)

Pecan

Macadamia
(culinary nut)

37

Sugar maple

Canada's sugar maple trees are tall and strong. Their sap is thickened into maple syrup.

Redwood

The tallest trees on Earth are the evergreen coastal redwoods of California. They can grow taller than the Statue of Liberty or Big Ben!

Kapok

Kapok trees are giants of the South American rainforests, towering above the canopy. They are drought deciduous— they lose their leaves in the dry season.

TREES AROUND THE WORLD

Trees are long-lived plants with a canopy of leaves at the top of a woody stem. They absorb pollution gases and release oxygen that we breathe. There are more than 60,000 species around the world.

Monkey puzzle

These ancient evergreens from Chile were dinosaur food during the Jurassic Period, 150 million years ago. They have spirals of triangular leaves.

There are no trees in Antarctica—it's too cold!

38

Oak

Oaks are large, mostly deciduous trees with leathery leaves. They have nuts, called acorns, which sit in little woody cups.

Silver birch

The silvery bark on these trees peels away like paper. Their thin leaf canopies let sunshine through, which plants beneath need to grow.

Ginkgo

These deciduous trees from China existed before dinosaurs! Some ginkgo fossils are more than 200 million years old.

Japanese cherry

The blossoms of these trees are a symbol of spring in Japan. Clouds of pink flowers are celebrated far and wide in a tradition known as Hanami.

African baobab

These trees live for thousands of years. Their barrel-like trunks store water so baobabs can produce fruit during the dry season, when few plants thrive.

Tree roots hold soil in place and soak up water.

Golden wattle

These Australian trees have yellow, sweet-smelling flowers. They grow wild in distant countries, such as Italy, after being carried overseas by humans.

RAINFOREST CANOPY

This tangled layer of leaves and branches, creepers and vines, is filled with tropical wildlife. There is more sunlight and rain here, high up above the forest floor.

Sticky pads on its toes help this frog cling to branches.

Hoffmann's two-toed sloth

A slow-moving sloth clings to branches with its long arms and hooked claws. It spends almost all its life upside down.

Red-eyed tree frog

This frog's green skin helps it blend in with its leafy surroundings. It flashes its red eyes and displays its orange feet to startle predators.

Orchids grow on branches, taking in nutrients and moisture from the air.

Insects

Many thousands of insect species live in the canopy layer. Scientists think there may be millions more species still to be discovered there!

Toucan

With its large beak, a toucan picks fruit from branches that are too small for it to stand on. It can also delve into tree holes and grab other birds' eggs.

The leaves of a bromeliad plant fan out around a cup-shaped center, which catches rainwater.

Howler monkeys

These monkeys start and end each day with a cacophony of deep howls. They are letting other howler monkeys know to stay away.

Lianas are thick, woody vines that climb up tree trunks, in search of sunlight.

Silky anteater

This nocturnal mammal is the world's smallest anteater. It can eat thousands of ants each night, then sleeps curled up in a ball during the day.

Higher and higher

Each layer of the rainforest offers a different habitat for animals and plants. Higher up there is plenty of sunlight, breeze, and rain. The forest floor is dark and damp.

Eyelash viper

This small, venomous snake has scales that stick out around its eyes, like eyelashes. It ambushes small animals, before gulping them down whole.

Emergent layer

Canopy

Understory

Forest floor

Cumulonimbus

Thundery cumulonimbus clouds are the tallest of all. They have dramatic, dark bottoms, thinner middles, and wide, lighter tops.

Cirrus

Wispy cirrus clouds look like locks of hair. They are formed by ice crystals high up, where the air is much colder.

Stratocumulus

Stratus clouds may spread out and break up to form puffy stripes of stratocumulus clouds, low in the sky.

CLOUD WATCHING

Clouds are made of tiny water droplets and ice crystals. They form when water vapor—water as a gas—cools and turns to liquid or ice. There are many different types of cloud...

Altostratus

A sheet of gray or bluish altostratus clouds cover most of the sky, at midlevel. The sun may glow softly through them.

Cirrocumulus

Rising and falling air makes rippled patterns— like fish scales. These small clouds are made of ice crystals and supercool liquid, high up in the sky.

Cumulus

These clouds look like soft, white cotton candy. They form lower down, where rising currents of warm, moist air first begin to cool.

Look for interesting shapes!

Noctilucent

Night-shining noctilucent clouds shimmer higher than any other clouds in the sky. They may appear just after sunset on clear summer evenings.

Stratus

A low, gray blanket of stratus clouds form when warmer, damp air breezes in after chilly weather. They often brings drizzle.

Upside down "rainbows"

These aren't really rainbows at all. They form when light refracts though ice crystals, high up in cirrus clouds. The scientific name is "circumzenithal arc."

Twinned rainbows

Twinned rainbows are very rare. No one is sure why they happen. Many scientists, however, think the light is refracted through water droplets that aren't spherical.

A double rainbow happens when there is a double reflection of light inside the water droplets.

Catching a rainbow

Rainbows only appear under the right conditions. The sun must be behind you and low in the sky, with water droplets in front of you.

Rainbows look arc-shaped from the ground, but they are actually full circles.

RAINBOWS

Sunlight travels in waves, which bounce and bend. It looks white, but is really made of all the colors of the rainbow.

Red rainbow

When the sun is on the horizon, blue and green light is scattered across the sky by Earth's atmosphere. This leaves yellows and reds to form a rainbow.

Fogbows

These ghostly looking arcs are formed by the tiny water droplets that make up fog. Fogbows are almost white, with only the faintest of colors visible.

Moonbows

Moonbows are rare lunar rainbows, made by moonlight. Our eyes see moonbows as almost white, even though all the colors are there very faintly.

How are rainbows formed?

When sunlight passes from air into a water droplet, it bends—or refracts. It bounces off the opposite side and refracts again as it passes out of the raindrop. As it refracts, it separates into different colors.

CLIFF FACE

The craggy face of a tall sea cliff reaches up into the air. Hardy plants and wildlife make their homes on rocky shelves and between the cracks.

Common lizard

A common lizard darts across the rock, seeking out a sheltered sunbathing spot. Lizards are cold-blooded, which means they need the sun's heat to stay warm.

The common lizard can shed its tail to distract an attacking predator.

Thrift

Stems of frilly, pink pom-poms sway above dense clumps of green. Thrift grows happily in nooks and on ledges, high up in the salty air.

Butterflies and moths are drawn to thrift for its sweet nectar.

Rock samphire is a tasty salty vegetable, but harvesting it is a dangerous job!

Rock samphire

Succulent rock samphire sprouts from crevices. It finds a way to hang on even when there is little soil.

Seabirds

Razorbills and other seabirds nest on cliff faces, keeping their eggs and chicks out of reach of predators, such as foxes. But gulls and ravens are still a threat.

A gannet circles above the sea, ready to plunge into the water and snatch a fish for supper.

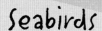

Razorbills

Gannets

Battered rock

Wind, rain, and powerful waves batter the rock, where high land meets the sea. Over time, the rock is worn away.

Waves smash the cliff with pebbles at great force. Small pieces of rock break away.

Stripes of rock

Cliffs can be striped with layers of red sandstone and white chalk, or other types of rock. The different layers form over millions of years, because of changing conditions on Earth.

Roseroot

Roseroot lights up shady crannies with its yellow flowers. These hardy plants can survive in freezing Arctic conditions.

WALL CLIMBERS

Up on a wall there is life between the bricks and mortar. Plants sprout, creep, and climb, while creatures, hide, nestle, or bask in the sunshine.

Zebra spiders are less than 0.4 in (1 cm) long, but they can jump as high as 4 in (10 cm)!

Honeysuckle

Zebra spider

This little striped, jumping spider stalks its prey across walls and fences. It creeps up on other small spiders, flies, and moths, then pounces.

Wisteria

Climbing plants

These plants sense when they brush against a wall or another plant to cling to. Many are vines, which grip a surface with twining tendrils, suckers, or clinging roots.

Ivy-leaved toadflax

Passionflower

Grape

Ivy-leaved toadflax

This flowering plant sows its own seeds in the crevices of walls. After pollination, the seed heads bend toward the wall to shed the seed.

In this tangle of ivy, a wren has made a nest.

Her long tail helps her balance.

Ivy

A good view

The top of a wall is a popular vantage point for cats. Instinctively, this feline feels safer high up, away from predators. She can watch for prey, too—look out little wren!

Moss

Mosses don't grow from seeds. Instead, they produce tiny spores. These cells are then carried off by the breeze.

When spores land on damp ground, tree bark, or a shaded bit of wall, new moss grows.

49

Birds of prey

Peregrines sometimes nest on tall buildings. They dive-bomb smaller birds at speeds of more than 200 mph (322 kph)!

ON THE ROOFTOPS

Above the streets of towns and cities, rooftops and other high spots can be safe places for urban animals. They rest or explore while people bustle below.

Far from home

Sometimes pets escape and learn to thrive in unexpected places. Wild rose-ringed parakeets come from tropical Africa and Asia, but they survive happily in cities such as London.

Scampering around

Racoons are skillful climbers, with strong claws for scaling trees. In towns they scamper onto roofs, ledges, and windowsills, in search of food.

Rich pickings

Racoons and foxes are not picky eaters. That's why they can be common in towns, where there are food scraps and trash to be raided after dark.

Sheltering animals

Some bats, such as pipistrelles, will squeeze themselves into holes and cracks under rooftops. Here, they shelter or hibernate during winter.

Pigeon

Rock dove

Urban cliffs

City pigeons huddle on high ledges, just as their wild relatives—rock doves—perch on cliffs. It is safer up there, away from predators on the ground—and easier to spot food!

A fox's bushy tail is often called a brush.

After dark

Red foxes can be seen in some cities when the sun goes down. They jump onto walls, scramble up fire escapes, and creep along fences, using their tails for balance.

Foxes are most active at dusk and dawn.

NOCTURNAL ANIMALS

Night falls and nocturnal animals begin to stir. As they fly through the air or scamper up branches, the darkness helps these creatures hide from predators and sneak up on prey.

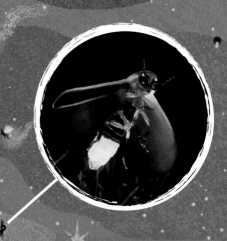

Fireflies

Fireflies are spots of brightness in the night sky. These small beetles use chemicals inside their bodies to make light. They flash brightly to attract a mate.

Flying squirrel

Many nocturnal animals have huge eyes with wide pupils, for letting in more light.

Large, cupped ears can pick up the slightest sound.

Townsend's big-eared bat

A keen sense of smell helps animals find food.

Opossum

Special Features

Nocturnal animals are active at night and rest during the day. The have evolved special traits, which help them find food and avoid predators in the dark.

Whiskers help nocturnal mammals feel their way through the darkness.

A barn owl's hearing is so good it can find prey in total darkness—even under snow.

Owls

Owls have large eyes for hunting in the dark. Their eyes don't move like ours do—instead, owls must swivel their heads to take a good look around.

An owl's head can rotate three-quarters of the way around its body!

Barn owl

Eastern screech owl

Great horned owl

Orb-weaver spiders

Orb-weaver spiders usually spin their webs at night to trap nocturnal insects. Some species tear them down at dawn and eat the silky threads so predators won't spot them.

BATS

Bats flit across the night sky on their agile wings. These flying mammals play an important part in keeping ecosystems healthy around the world.

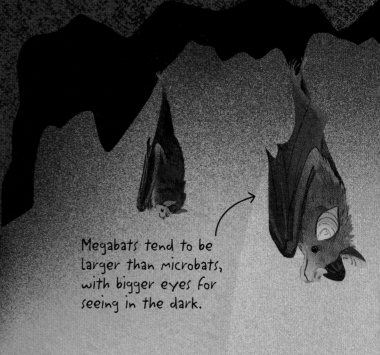

Megabats tend to be larger than microbats, with bigger eyes for seeing in the dark.

Bat groups

Bats can be divided into two groups—megabats and microbats. Megabats feed on fruit, nectar, and pollen. Microbats eat insects and use echolocation to navigate.

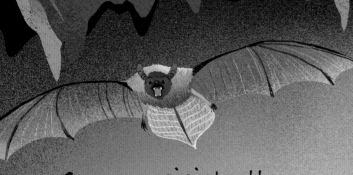

Common pipistrelle

The pipistrelle feeds on gnats, flies, and mosquitoes across most of Europe and North Africa. It can feast on up to 3,000 insects in one night!

Bats hang upside down so they can easily fly away.

Roosting

Bats often live and rest together in large groups. This is called roosting. Bats roost in dark crevices, such as in caves and trees, and under rooftops, hanging upside down.

Dinnertime

Some medium-sized microbats feed on small frogs and lizards as well as insects. In Central and South America, vampire bats sip blood from birds, cattle, and horses.

Bumblebee bat

This bat from Thailand is the size of a bumblebee! It's the smallest mammal in the world, weighing no more than half a teaspoon of sugar.

Bumblebee bats can hover like hummingbirds (see page 21).

Giant golden-crowned flying fox

This is one of the world's biggest bats. Its wingspan is wider than your outstretched arms! It lives in the Philippines and feasts on figs.

Bats are the only mammals that can fly.

Pollination

Megabats are useful pollinators. Some fruit trees, such as bananas and mangos, are pollinated by megabats as they flit from tree to tree, supping nectar from the blossom.

Echolocation

Microbats send out high-pitched sounds, which bounce back off objects around them. The echoes help bats find their way and locate their insect prey.

Saguaro cacti flowers bloom for one night only. They are pollinated by lesser long-nosed bats.

55

Waxing gibbous

More than half of the illuminated side of the moon is visible. It is still waxing.

First quarter

Half of the sunlit portion of the moon is in view. We see a half-moon.

Waxing crescent

A thin crescent is visible in the sky. It is waxing, which means it is getting bigger each night.

The expression "once in a blue moon" comes from the rare event of two full moons in one month.

New moon

The moon is lined up between the sun and the Earth. The side facing Earth is in darkness, so we can't see the moon at all.

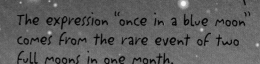
The moon makes a full orbit of the Earth in just under a month.

MOON PHASES

The moon seems to change shape as it orbits (moves around) the Earth. Actually, it is just our view that is changing, as the sun lights up different parts of the moon's surface.

Waning gibbous

More than half of the illuminated side of the moon is visible. It is waning, or getting smaller, now.

Third quarter

Half of the illuminated portion of the moon is in view. This phase is the opposite side compared with the first quarter.

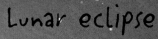

Waning crescent

A thin crescent is visible. It is waning night by night.

Full moon

Our view is of the entire sunlit side of the moon. Every three years or so, there is a second full moon in a month.

Lunar eclipse

When the Earth lines up between the sun and the moon, it casts a shadow over the moon's surface, which makes the moon look red.

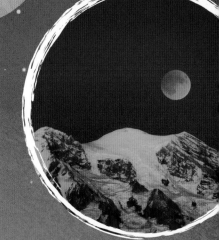

There are eight distinct phases of the moon to spot in the night sky.

Supermoon

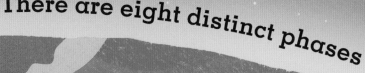

When a full moon happens at the closest point to Earth in the moon's orbit, it looks especially big and bright. We call this a supermoon.

CONSTELLATIONS

We call clusters of bright stars constellations. People once used them to map out the night sky, to navigate, and to track the time of year. Here are some constellations to look for.

Star Finding

Constellations can help us recognize individual stars. The North Star, or Polaris, can be found by tracing a straight line from the Big Dipper.

North Star

Ursa Minor

Sailors once used the North Star's height to figure out their position at sea.

A different view

The Northern and Southern Hemispheres (the halves of the Earth) have different views of the sky. The constellations appear in different places, or are nowhere to be seen! This is a section of the northern sky.

The Ancient Greeks named many constellations after mythical beings.

Southern sky

Crux

Teapot

Boötes

This constellation's name means "the herdsman." It contains one of the brightest stars in the night sky, Arcturus, which blazes a red-orange color.

Some constellations, such as Sagittarius, can be seen on the other side of the world during certain months.

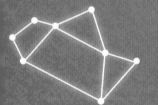
Sagittarius

Scorpius

Canis Major

Capricornus

Libra

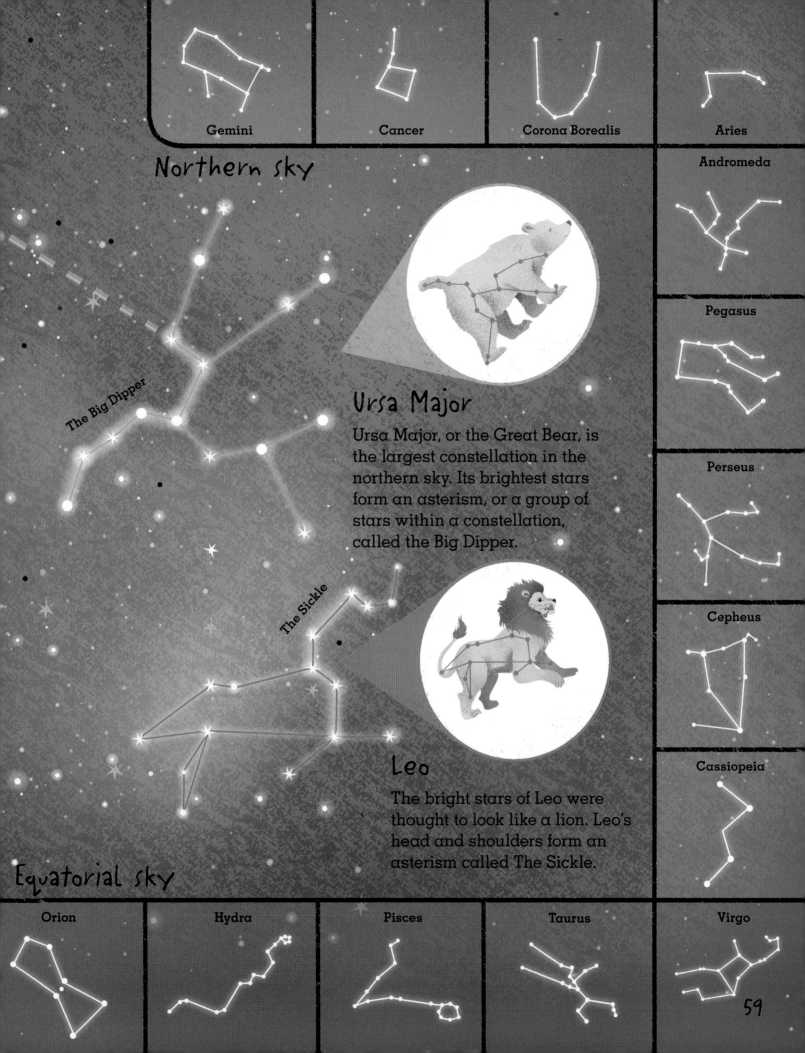

Gemini

Cancer

Corona Borealis

Aries

Andromeda

Northern sky

Pegasus

Perseus

The Big Dipper

Ursa Major

Ursa Major, or the Great Bear, is the largest constellation in the northern sky. Its brightest stars form an asterism, or a group of stars within a constellation, called the Big Dipper.

Cepheus

The Sickle

Cassiopeia

Leo

The bright stars of Leo were thought to look like a lion. Leo's head and shoulders form an asterism called The Sickle.

Equatorial sky

Orion

Hydra

Pisces

Taurus

Virgo

59

GLOSSARY

air pressure
Weight of air pushing against objects

airborne
Carried by the air

atmosphere
Layer of gases around a planet

bird of prey
Bird that hunts other animals for food

cell
Basic building block of all living things

constellation
Group of stars that form a pattern in the sky

deciduous
Tree that loses its leaves in winter

ecosystem
An environment and all the living things within it that depend on each other for food, pollination, and more

environment
Everything that surrounds us. Home to plants and animals

Equator
Imaginary line around the middle of the Earth, between the North and South Pole

fertile
Suitable for growing things

gas
Substance that has no fixed shape, such as oxygen in the air

global warming
An increase in Earth's temperatures over a long period of time

insect
Living thing with a body made up of three parts— a head, middle, and end section

mammal
Warm-blooded animal, with a backbone and fur or hair, that usually gives birth to babies rather than lays eggs

microbe
Tiny organism, such as a bacterium, that can often only be seen with a microscope

navigation

How an animal finds its way around

nocturnal

Active at night

nutrient

Chemical used by living things to help them grow and stay healthy

organism

Living thing

particle

Tiny part of something, such as dust or a fragment of pollen

photosynthesis

Process plants use to make their food

pollination

How flowering plants reproduce

pollution

Harmful substances in the environment, such as a gas or particles that make the air less healthy

predator

Animal that hunts other animals for food

prey

Animal that is eaten by another animal

rainforest

Tall forest with a lot of rain

reproduce

When a living thing produces young

season

Period of similar weather caused by Earth's position in its orbit around the sun

seed

Beginning of a new plant, encased in a protective cover

species

Group of similar animals or plants. For example, all dogs are a single species

venomous

Type of creature that releases a harmful substance through a bite or sting

water vapor

Water in the form of a gas

INDEX

ACKNOWLEDGMENTS

Zoë would like to thank: Super-editor Kat Teece for bringing all of this together, Philip Armstrong for his excellent physics advice, and Alice Williams for being an all-round fantastic agent.

DK would like to thank: Marie Greenwood for her editorial help, Polly Goodman for proofreading the book, Helen Peters for the index, and the publishing team at Royal Botanic Gardens, Kew, for their advice about plants.

The publisher would like to thank the following for their kind permission to reproduce their photographs:

(Key: a-above; b-below/bottom; c-centre; f-far; l-left; r-right; t-top)

4 123RF.com: Vasiliy Vishnevskiy (cb). **Alamy Stock Photo:** Tim Plowden (cr). **Shutterstock.com:** Lucid Formation (clb). **6 Alamy Stock Photo**: imageBROKER (cla). **7 Dorling Kindersley:** Natural History Museum, London (ca). **Fotolia:** Eric Isselee (c). **10 Dreamstime.com:** Corinazone (ca). **12 Alamy Stock Photo:** All Canada Photos (cl). **Dreamstime.com:** Feathercollector (b). **13 Alamy Stock Photo:** Amazon-Images (c); Papilio (cla); INSADCO Photography (bl). **15 Dreamstime.com:** Andreykuzmin (ca). **16 123RF.com:** Richard E Leighton Jr (cra); Thawat Tanhai (cla). **18 Alamy Stock Photo:** David Plummer (tc). **Dorling Kindersley:** Thomas Marent (bl); Natural History Museum, London (cr). **Dreamstime.com:** Fotofred (cla). **19 Alamy Stock Photo:** Robert Pickett / Papilio (cra). **Dorling Kindersley:** Natural History Museum, London (tl); Natural History Museum (bl). **Dreamstime.com:** Acharaporn Kamornboonyarush (cl). **20 Alamy Stock Photo:** GTW / imageBROKER (bc); Glenn Bartley / All Canada Photos (ca); UDAZKENA (cb). **21 Alamy Stock Photo:** Steven Blandin (cb); Tom Langlands Photography (tr); Glenn Bartley / All Canada Photos (c); Sense2 (bl). **22 Alamy Stock Photo:** B.A.E. Inc. (cra); Doug Lindstrand / Design Pics Inc (tc); Paul R. Sterry / Nature Photographers Ltd (crb). **Dreamstime.com:** Delmas Lehman (cla). **23 Alamy Stock Photo:** Juniors Bildarchiv / F312 / Juniors Bildarchiv GmbH (tl); Volker Lautenbach / imageBROKER (cra); Manjeet & Yograj Jadeja (cb). **25 Dreamstime.com:** Sander Meertins (tc). **26 Alamy Stock Photo:** William Leaman (tc); Kristo Robert (crb). **27 Alamy Stock Photo:** Prakash Chandra (crb). **Dorling Kindersley:** Natural History Museum, London (cb). **Dreamstime.com:** Fazle Abbas (cr). **28 123RF.com:** Sergio_Ksv (c). **29 Alamy Stock Photo:** Greg C Grace (bl). **Dreamstime.com:** Hudakore (cra); Ievgenii Tryfonov (tl). **30 123RF.com:** Alein (crb); Eric Isselee / isselee (bl). **Fotolia:** Eric Isselee (c); maxcom (cra). **31 123RF.com:** Eric Isselee / isselee (cra). **Dorling Kindersley:** British Wildlife Centre, Surrey, UK (cl). **Dreamstime.com:** Isselee (tl). **Fotolia:** Eric Isselee (crb). **35 Alamy Stock Photo:** Konrad Wothe / naturepl.com (tr); Janet Griffin-Scott (cl). **36 Dreamstime.com:** Mahira (tc). **37 Alamy Stock Photo:** www.pqpictures.co.uk (tr). **38 Alamy Stock Photo:** Clynt Garnham (cb). **Dreamstime.com:** Aoldman (c); Melinda Fawver (tc). **Getty Images / iStock:** Nirian (ca). **39 Alamy Stock Photo:** Stephanie Jackson - Aust wildflower collection (crb); Thorsten Negro / imageBROKER (cl); Frank Teigler / Premium Stock Photography GmbH (ca); Frank Sommariva / imageBROKER (c); Alex Segre (cra). **Dreamstime.com:** Enticksnap (cla). **40 Alamy Stock Photo:** Kalmi / Panther Media GmbH (cl); Anton Sorokin (bl); Nodramallama (tr); Glenn Bartley / All Canada Photos (crb). **41 Alamy Stock Photo:** Amazon-Images (cra); Zizza Gordon - Panama Wildlife (c); Francesco Puntiroli (clb). **42 Alamy Stock Photo:** Alan Dyer / Stocktrek Images (br). **Getty Images / iStock:** MRRTxPilot (tc). **46 Alamy Stock Photo:** Krystyna Szulecka Photography (bc); Tony Peacock (c). **47 Alamy Stock Photo:** Photimageon (clb). **48 Alamy Stock Photo:** Scenics & Science (tl). **49 Alamy Stock Photo:** blickwinkel / Hecker (tl); Ian McGlasham (tr); Andrew Walmsley (ca); Michael Piepgras (bl). **50 Alamy Stock Photo:** Frank Hecker (bl). **51 Alamy Stock Photo:** Gregorius Krisna Adhi / EyeEm (tc); Michael Clark / FLPA / imageBROKER (cla); Toby Houlton (tr). **52 Alamy Stock Photo:** Phil Degginger (tr); Joe McDonald / Steve Bloom Images (cl); Mansell, Barry / SuperStock (cb); Ivan Kuzmin (br). **53 123RF.com:** Evelyn Harrison (cra). **Alamy Stock Photo:** Dominique Braud / Dembinsky Photo Associates (cb); Piumatti Sergio / Prisma by Dukas Presseagentur GmbH (cl); Rosanne Tackaberry (c). **57 Alamy Stock Photo:** Dorset Media Service (bl); Kevin Ebi (cr).

All other images © Dorling Kindersley
For further information see: www.dkimages.com